WHAT IS LIGHTNING?

Mc Graw Hill **SRA**

Columbus, OH

SRAonline.com

 SRA

The *McGraw·Hill* Companies

The sky lights up. You hear a rumble. It is lightning! Did you know that lightning is energy? It is a kind of electricity.

Long ago people thought that lightning was mysterious. Ben Franklin was a scientist from long ago. He wanted to learn about lightning.

Franklin made a plan. He thought lightning would hit a metal key. He used string to tie the key to a kite.

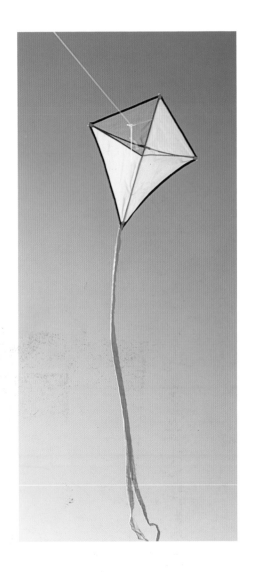

Franklin went outside in a storm. He flew the kite and key. He knew it was not safe. He was very careful.

Lightning hit the key! The string was trembling. Franklin learned something new. He learned that lightning is electricity.

Franklin was brave. He was not afraid to learn
new things. Next he had to inform people about
what he learned.

Franklin told people about his test. Other scientists learned from Franklin. They did tests too. One scientist made the first light bulb!

Now we use electricity for many things. We use it for computers. We use it to turn on lights. Franklin would be very happy. His courage helped us all.

Vocabulary

rumble (rum' bəl) (page 3) *n.* A heavy, deep, rolling sound.

mysterious (mis tēr' ē əs) (page 4) *adj.* Difficult to understand or explain.

trembling (trem' bling) (page 7) A form of the verb **tremble:** To shake.

brave (brāv) (page 8) *adj.* Not afraid.

afraid (ə frād') (page 8) *adj.* Feeling fear.

inform (in fôrm') (page 8) *v.* To tell.

courage (kûr' ij) (page 10) *n.* The strength to overcome fear.

Comprehension Focus: Cause and Effect

1. What caused the string on the kite to tremble?

2. Why did Franklin tell other people about his invention?

Activity: Thinking About Electricity

Do this activity to see how Ben Franklin helped us all!

What to Do

1. Talk with a partner about ways to use electricity.
2. Make a poster with your partner. Use words and pictures. Write ways to use electricity. Cut out pictures that show ways to use electricity. Glue them onto your poster. You can draw pictures too!

What You Need

- Posterboard
- Markers
- Safety scissors
- Magazines
- Glue

What Happened

- What are different ways to use electricity?
- Which things on your poster do you use most?

What If

What if we did not have electricity? How would life be different?